SKIPPER'S EYE VIEW

of the West Indies

Hand drawn by Capt. W.S.M. Brown, DSO, OBE, DSC, RN ret.
1967-68

Published by

Shipyard Press
Miami

SKIPPER'S EYE VIEW

Copyright 2011 by Shipyard Press
www.shipyardpress.com

ʃP

ISBN Print Edition 978-0-9769903-9-0

Published by Shipyard Press
Printed in the United States of America

For quantity purchases of this publication please see Shipyard Press website:
www.shipyardpress.com

FOREWORD

Captain Bruno Brown was in love with the Caribbean. This book is a testament to his life and work there. Although, we share a common name, I knew him only by sight and reputation. We spoke only once, while tending our boats during hurricane David. Re-publishing his handiwork is the best way I know to honor his contributions to the islands and their people.

I was given an original copy of this book by my friend and mentor,
Captain Fergus (Fergie) Walker,
who wrote this advice on the cover, "Read this and you will know more than...."

Using Capt. Bruno's book, and Capt. Walker's advice, I tried to give my charter guests an experience they would treasure the rest of their lives. We would often sail off the beaten path between the islands, sometimes anchoring away from other charter boats, and generally try to explore, both on land and underwater, the many unusual, interesting and sometimes scary places of the islands and reefs.

I fondly treasure the friendship and community of charter skippers who sailed with me, a swashbuckling group of highly independent, very competent sailors, responsible for making these islands the vacation destinations they have become. Using their yachts, as elegant floating hotels, they opened up many islands, where there had been few shoreside establishments catering to tourists. In many ways the economic progress and tourist development of the Virgin Islands, St.Martin, Antigua, St. Kitts, St. Lucia and the Grenadines occurred, following the wakes of yacht chartering in the Caribbean.

I hope you enjoy this look at some golden days of chartering in the Islands, and treasure Capt. Bruno's gems of knowledge from a day gone, but not forgotten. Most of his advice recorded here, is valid yet today.

Capt. Conrad N. Brown, Jr.

"SKIPPER'S EYE VIEW"

OF THE WEST INDIES

"Read This And You Will Know More Than"

RECTUB AGIT

SEMPER

EMPTOR

CAPT. FERGUS WALKER

P. O. Box 3918
St. Thomas, U.S.V.I. 00801

Bruce Brown

INDEX

EDITORS NOTE:

Cdr. W.S.M. (Bruno) Brown DSO, OBE, DSC, RN (ret)
the author and illustrator of this pamphlet
originally prepared it for yacht charterers
based on his almost ten years of cruising in
these waters. The information in it, however,
appears to be of general interest to all those
enjoying this delightful area, whether on
land, cruise ships, or "island hopping" by air.

OUR CRUISING AREA

WITH THE EASTCOAST OF AMERICA SUPER-IMPOSED ON THE SAME SCALE

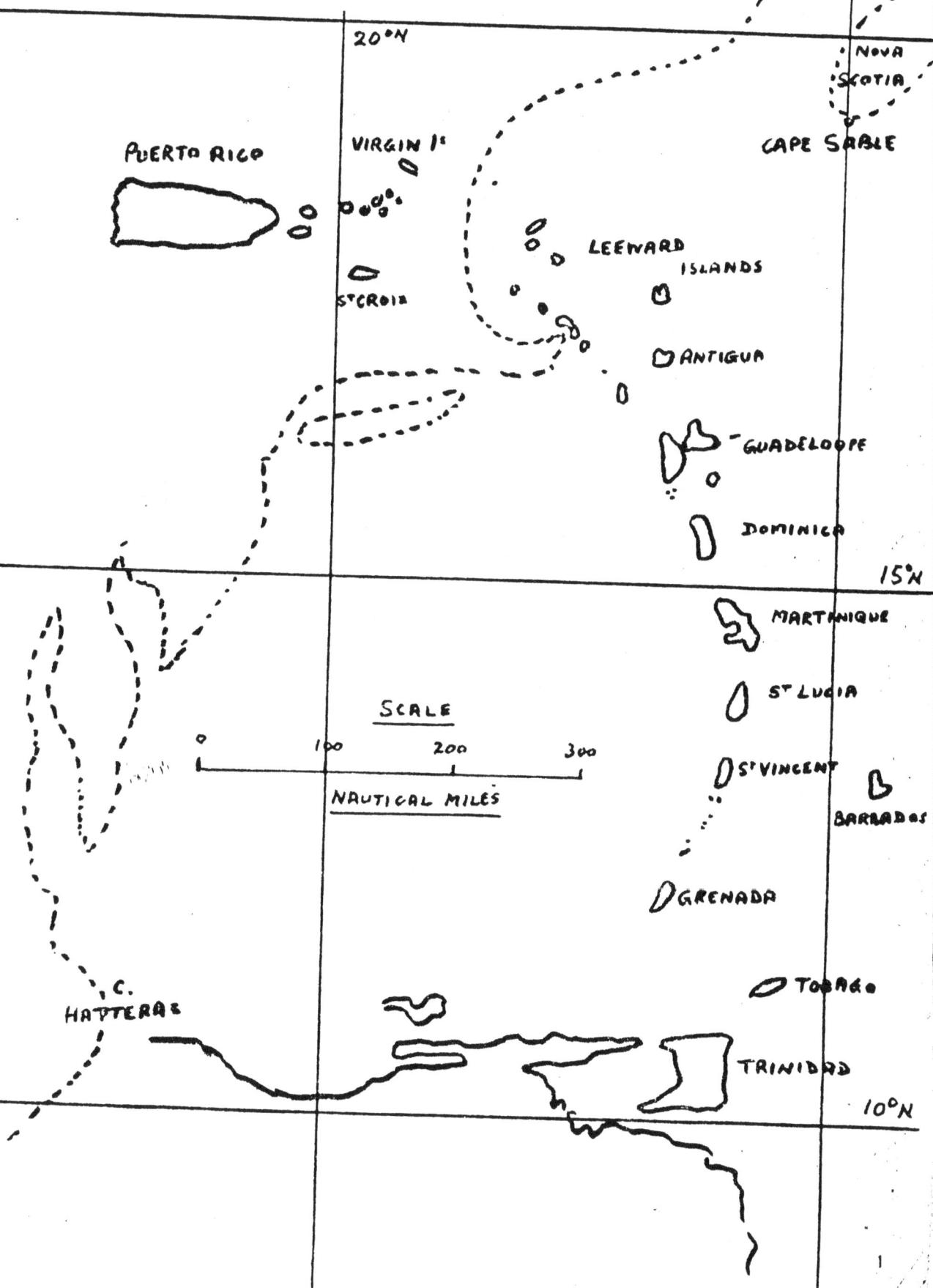

20°N

NOVA SCOTIA

CAPE SABLE

PUERTO RICO

VIRGIN I^s

LEEWARD ISLANDS

St CROIX

ANTIGUA

GUADELOUPE

DOMINICA

15°N

MARTINIQUE

SCALE

0   100   200   300

NAUTICAL MILES

St LUCIA

St VINCENT

BARBADOS

GRENADA

TOBAGO

C. HATTERAS

TRINIDAD

10°N

SPORTING EQUIPMENT.

IN A BLINDING GLIMPSE OF THE OBVIOUS, ONE MIGHT SAY THAT THE PEOPLE WHO ENJOY CRUISING HERE MOST, ARE THOSE WHO ENJOY THE THINGS THAT CRUISING HERE MOST NATURALLY PROVIDES. AND CONVERSELY, THAT THE PEOPLE WHO ARE MOST LIKELY TO BE DISAPPOINTED, ARE THOSE WHO EXPECT IT TO PROVIDE SOMETHING ELSE.

WHAT DOES CRUISING HERE NOT PROVIDE ?

GOLF OR TENNIS FOR A START. IT IS SIMPLY NOT WORTH BRINGING THE EQUIPMENT FOR THE FEW OPPORTUNITIES THAT YOU WILL GET.

FISHING IS IN A DIFFERENT CATEGORY. WE USUALLY CATCH QUITE ENOUGH FISH FOR THE TABLE, BUT BY VERY SIMPLE METHODS. BUT THE "MAD-ABOUT-FISHING" ENTHUSIAST, ARMED TO THE TEETH FROM THE ARSENALS OF ABERCROMBIE AND FITCH, SELDOM SEEMS TO HAVE HIS SKILL REWARDED, AND IS APT TO REGRET HIS EXCESS BAGGAGE. OUR FISH HAVE NOT BEEN PROPERLY EDUCATED, PERHAPS.

NIGHT-LIFE AND WATER-SKIING ALSO FLOURISH MORE LUXURIANTLY ELSEWHERE.

ON THE OTHER HAND :-

THE SWIMMING HERE IS WONDERFUL, PARTICULARLY UNDER WATER. SCUBA GEAR IS UNNECESSARY. IT IS DIFFICULT AND EXPENSIVE TO PROVIDE, AND THOSE WHO ASK FOR IT SELDOM USE IT. JUST PLAIN SCHNORKELLING AROUND THE CORAL REEFS IS IDEAL HERE. MASKS AND SCHNORKELS WE CAN PROVIDE, BUT FINS ARE MORE DIFFICULT. FINS, LIKE SHOES MUST FIT. IT WOULD BE IMPOSSIBLE TO KEEP ON BOARD ENOUGH FINS TO FIT EVERYBODY'S SIZES.

PHOTOGRAPHY. EVERYTHING YOU SEE OR DO ON A CRUISE HERE IS MADLY PHOTOGENIC. SO DO COME WELL EQUIPPED. AS THE LIGHT IS PERFECT FOR PHOTOGRAPHY, THE SIMPLEST GEAR IS BEST : IT DOESN'T BREAK DOWN SO OFTEN, AND YOU MAY EVEN BE ABLE TO BUY ITS FILMS HERE.

"IF YOU HAVE A MOMENT AFTER THE NEXT RUBBER, WE DO HAPPEN TO BE PASSING ONE OF THE BEAUTY SPOTS OF THE WORLD".

FILMS

I AM AFRAID IT IS ALREADY TOO LATE TO WARN YOU THAT YOU HAVE
BROUGHT TOO FEW FILMS FOR YOUR CAMERA.
FILMS ARE NOT EASY TO GET AROUND HERE.
ON THE TOURIST ROUTE — SOMETIMES — PERHAPS.
BUT WHERE WE MAINLY GO —
NEVER.

SO, STOCK UP WHEREVER YOU CAN TO THE REQUIRED QUOTA.
THE QUOTA IS CALCULATED LIKE THIS:—
"THINK OF A NUMBER OF FILMS THAT YOU COULDN'T POSSIBLY USE IN
THE TIME, HOWEVER HARD YOU TRIED.
DOUBLE THIS NUMBER.
ADD A FEW FOR LUCK "
YOU MIGHT FIND THIS JUST ENOUGH.

WHERE ARE WE ?

CHICAGO

CANADA

HALIFAX

NEW YORK

40°

35°

σ BERMUDA

30°

MIAMI

25°

HAVANA

20°

σ ANTIGUA

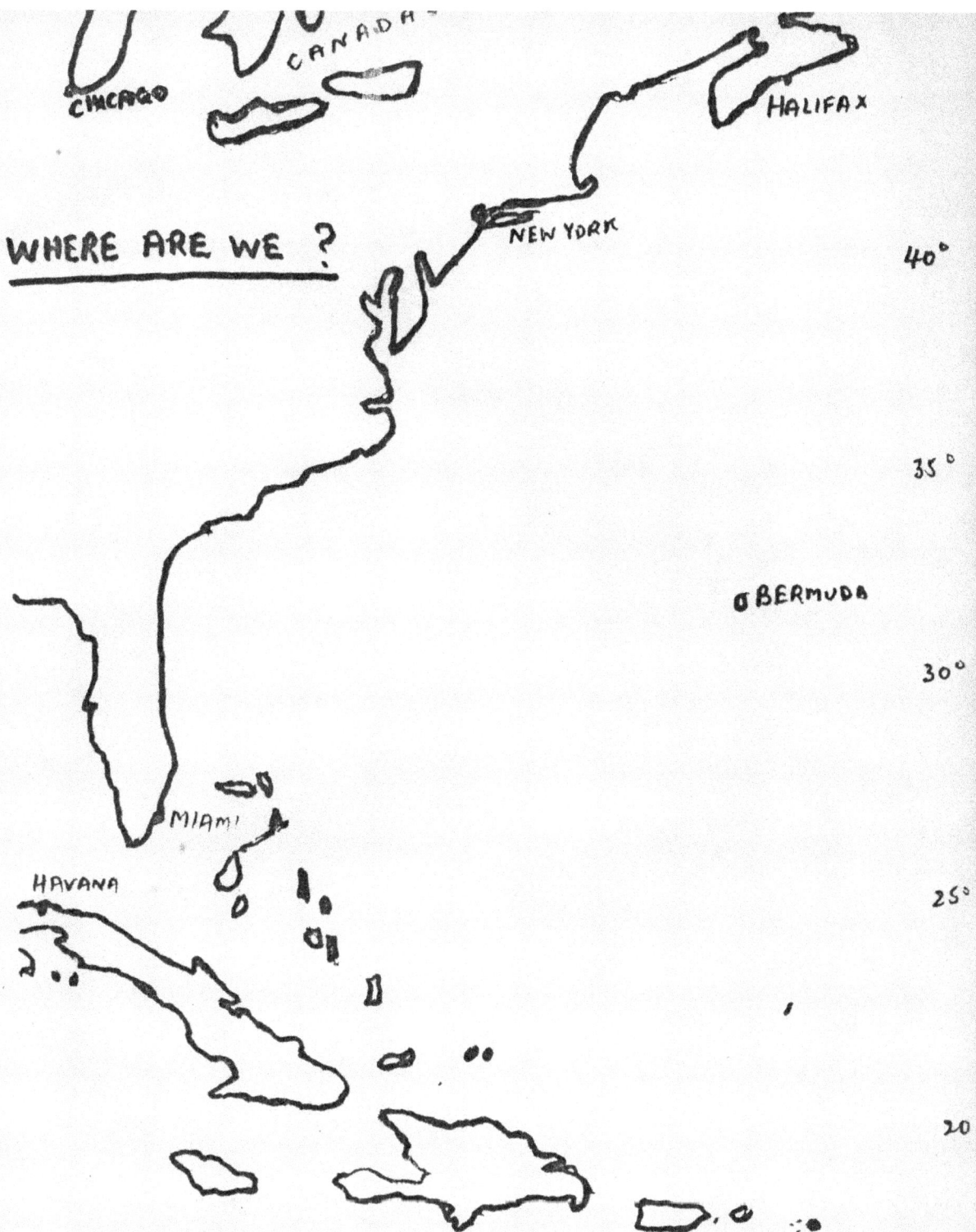

DID YOU REALISE THAT :-

y. ANTIGUA IS EQUIDISTANT FROM :-
   (a) MIAMI   (b) NEW YORK And (c) HALIFAX ?

2/ CASTRO IN HAVANA LIVES CLOSER TO YOU THAN TO US ?

THESE FACTS ARE INFORMATIVE, SURPRISING AND ALMOST TRUE.

15

75°   70°   65°   5

RECURRENT NAMES

PITON
LITERALLY "SPIKE" AS IN ONES
RUNNING SHOES. FIGURATIVELY
HERE FOR SPIKY MOUNTAINS

MORNE
LITERALLY "GLOOMY"
USED LOCALLY FOR
HILLS WHICH ARE
NOT QUITE MOUNTAINS

ANSE   A SMALL BAY OR COVE.
A BAYE IS MUCH BIGGER

CUL-DE-SAC   LITERALLY   BOTTOM OF THE SACK. A BLIND ALLEY.
CUL-DE-SAC. MARIN — A NAUTICAL BLIND ALLEY.

SOUFRIERE
LITERALLY A SULPHUR SPRING.
ALSO USED AS TOWN AND
MOUNTAIN NAMES.

MARIGOT   MEANS A PARTIALLY ENCLOSED BAY WHERE FRESH
AND SALT WATER MEET.

CODRINGTON   A COLONIAL ADMINISTRATOR WHO HAD A
FLAIR FOR GETTING HIS NAME ON THE MAP.

HAUT AND BASSE   NOT SO MUCH "HIGH AND LOW" IN ALTITUDE
BUT RATHER "UP AND DOWN" WIND.

cf BASSE TERRE, GUADELOUPE WHICH IS MOUNTAINOUS BUT DOWN WIND
and TERRE d'EN HAUT, SAINTES, WHICH IS NOT HIGH, BUT IS UP WIND.

"CAN I WEAR SHORTS ASHORE, OR MUST I WEAR A TIE?"

THE ONLY ACTUAL RULES ON THE SUBJECT ARE MADE BY SOME HOTELS WHICH REQUIRE JACKETS AND TIES FOR DINNER.

OTHERWISE IT IS LEFT TO COMMON SENSE. I HAVE ONLY KNOWN OF TWO CASES IN WHICH PEOPLE HAVE BEEN ORDERED OFF THE STREETS.

IN THE HEART OF THE TOURIST ROUTE ALMOST ANYTHING GOES — ALMOST UNNOTICED. YOU COULDN'T START TO COMPETE WITH EVEN THE AVERAGE.

BUT OFF THE TOURIST ROUTE — AND MOST OF THE PLACES WE VISIT ARE OFF IT — MY BEST ADVICE IS TO DRESS JUST AS YOU WOULD ON A SUMMER'S DAY IN THE CORRESPONDING SORT OF PLACE AT HOME.

NOBODY HERE IS "OFFENDED" BY THIS SORT OF FANCY DRESS. THEY JUST THINK IT IS COMIC, AND IF YOU LIKE TO BE A FIGURE OF FUN ....

BE CAREFUL ABOUT TAKING PHOTOGRAPHS OF PEOPLE IN THEIR WORKING CLOTHES. THEY MAY LOOK PICTURESQUE TO YOU. BUT THEY MAY NOT LIKE IT. "SUPERSTITION" YOU SAY.! "BOLONY!" SAY I.

HOW WOULD YOU LIKE IT IF SOME CANDID-CAMERAMAN (AND COLOURED AT THAT) BURST INTO YOUR KITCHEN WHEN YOU WERE DOING YOUR MORNING CHORES: WITH YOUR HAIR IN CURLERS, AND YOUR FACE NOT MADE UP. HE MIGHT THINK YOU PICTURESQUE TOO, BUT WOULD YOUR OBJECTIONS BE SUPERSTITION.

TAXIS

LETS FACE IT !

TAXIS ARE EXPENSIVE HERE.
MUCH MORE SO THAN THEY
ARE AT HOME.

BUT CAN YOU WONDER
WHEN YOU EXPERIENCE
OUR EXCRABLE ROADS,
WHICH SHAKE A CAR TO
PIECES IN NO TIME.

YOU WILL NOTICE THAT
MOST OF THE TAXIS ARE
ALMOST BRAND NEW, AND
THAT THEY ARE ALREADY
FALLING TO PIECES.

REMEMBER ALSO THAT OUR TAXI OWNERS AND DRIVERS HAVE TO MAKE A
YEARS LIVING OUT OF A FOUR MONTH SEASON.
THE MORE REMOTE THE PLACE YOU VISIT, THE MORE DOES THIS ALL APPLY. IN
MARTINIQUE, WHERE THE ROADS ARE BETTER, CARS LAST LONGER AND THE TAXIS
ARE OLDER.
SO BE BRAVE ! THE TAXIS WON'T COST YOU MUCH MORE THAN YOU SAVE
ON THE LOW COST OF LIQUOR ONBOARD. AND ANYHOW, TO GET THE FULL
ENJOYMENT OUT OF YOUR CRUISE, YOU MUST GET AROUND AND SEE THE
ISLANDS. YOU MISS HALF THE FUN BY STAYING IN SIGHT OF THE LANDING
PLACE, JUST AS YOU WOULD ANYWHERE ELSE.

WHEN I RECOMMEND A TAXI DRIVER, IT HAS NOTHING TO DO WITH THE
PRICE, EITHER ONE WAY OR THE OTHER. IT IS BECAUSE I KNOW HIM TO BE A
GOOD GUIDE WHO WILL STRIKE THE DELICATE BALANCE BETWEEN POINTING
OUT THINGS AND FACTS THAT YOU MIGHT OTHERWISE MISS, AND BORING
YOU WITH INTERMINABLE CHATTER. MANY OF THE TAXI DRIVERS ARE
EXCELLENT GUIDES IN THIS RESPECT AND THEIR SERVICES ARE
INVALUABLE TO YOU. YOU WILL LEARN ABOUT LOCAL POLITICS FROM THEM,
ABOUT LOCAL CUSTOMS, AND THE WAY PEOPLE THINK IN THESE ISLANDS.
THESE THINGS ARE JUST AS MUCH A PART OF THE CRUISE, AND SOMETHING
TO TAKE BACK WITH YOU, AS A SUN TAN OR A FUNNY STRAW HAT. AND THESE
THINGS YOU CAN ONLY GET FROM YOUR TAXI DRIVERS.

VEGETABLES

ROOTS

TUBERS

SWEET POTATOES AND YAMS

DACHINE (BIG) TANYA (SMALL)   EDDOES.

EDDOES ARE CLUSTERS OF SMALL ROOTS AROUND A PARENT ROOT. EDDOE LEAVES ARE ALSO GOOD TO EAT.

ON VINES

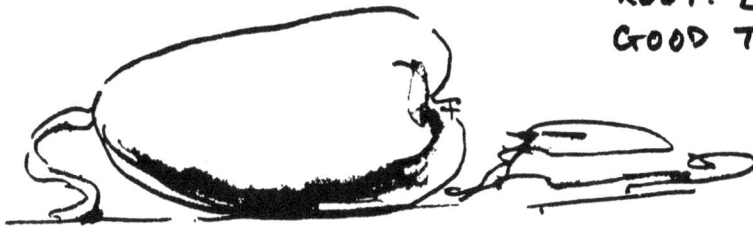

CHRISTOPHINE (WHITE)
TABLE SQUASH (GREEN)
CUCUMBERS
PUMPKIN
WATER MELON
MUSK MELON

ON BUSHES

EGG PLANT

FRUIT

PINEAPPLE.   DID YOU KNOW THAT IT GROWS THIS WAY UP AND THIS CLOSE TO THE GROUND ?

9

FRUIT

BREAD FRUIT
(USED AS A VEGITABLE)
BEAUTIFUL TO LOOK AT

SOURSOP

UGLY AS SIN.

GREEN PRICKLY SKIN
WHITE SOFT FLESH . DELICIOUS
WHEN SQUASHED AS A COLD DRINK.

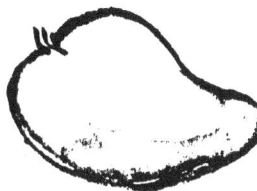

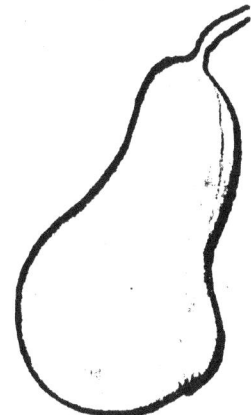

SAPADILLO

HARD BROWN SKIN
A FEW LARGE BLACK PIPS..
TASTES LIKE ... SAPERDILLO

MANGO

CALABASH

NOT EATEN AT ALL.

ON "SORT OF" TREES

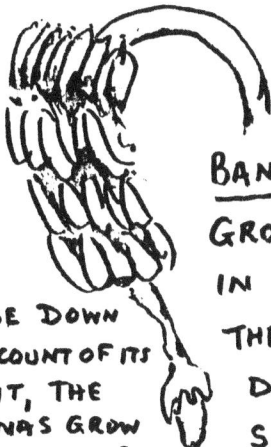

BANANAS

GROW AND RIPEN
IN A FEW MONTHS.
THE "TREE" THEN
DIES AND A NEW
SHOOT SPRINGS
FROM THE ROOT.

UPSIDE DOWN
ON ACCOUNT OF ITS
WEIGHT, THE
BANANAS GROW
UP INSTEAD OF
HANGING DOWN.

PAU·PAU (W.I.)
(OR PAPAYA)

A SOFT PULPWOOD
"TREE". WITH NO
BRANCHES

EATING MANGOS

WHAT'S ALL THIS FUSS ABOUT EATING MANGOS
AND THE CORNY OLD JOKE ABOUT HAVING TO
DO SO IN YOUR BATH!

IF YOU WERE LUCKY ENOUGH
TO BE A WEST INDIAN, YOU
WOULD HAVE NO PROBLEM AT ALL.

AS YOU ARE NOT, START BY
STUDYING THE ANATOMY OF THE
MANGO. IT IS A FLAT, OVAL FRUIT
WITH A FLAT, OVAL STONE REACHING
ALMOST FROM SIDE TO SIDE.

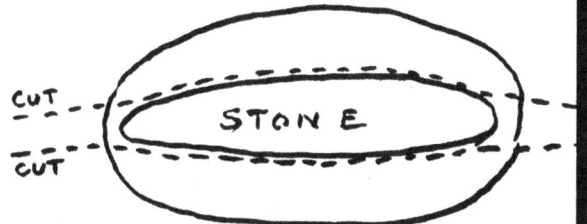

CUT

STONE

CUT

THIS CROSS SECTION SHOULD SHOW
YOU WHERE TO CUT.

IT RESULTS IN A TOP
AND A BOTTOM
CONTAINING MOST
OF THE FLESH, WHICH
CAN BE POLITELY REMOV
WITH A SPOON.
THE MIDDLE SECTION IS
ALMOST ALL STONE AND
CAN BE POLITELY
DISREGARD

NO TROUBLE AT ALL !!
NO NONSENSE ABOUT A BATH !
(JUST A QUICK SHOWER WILL DO)

11

CENTURY PLANT
SOME SAY IT LIVES 100 YEARS.

OR DAGGER PLANT
ITS LEAVES ARE LIKE DAGGERS.

OR MAY POLE
IT BLOSSOMS IN MAY.

FOR MANY YEARS THE CENTURY PLANT GROWS HARD AND STRONG. A BUNCH OF DAGGERS, IT HAS A FIERCE BEAUTY, BUT IS TOTALLY DEVOID OF CHARM. THAT IS HOW MOST PEOPLE SEE IT.

THEN SUDDENLY IN THE SPRINGTIME, IN THE MONTH OF MAY, ONE PLANT AFTER ANOTHER ERUPTS IN ONE FINAL MONTH OF GLORY.

FIRST, A GREAT GREEN POLE THRUSTS ITSELF 20 FEET INTO THE SKY AND ON TOP OF THIS A GOLDEN SHOWER OF BLOSSOM BURSTS FORTH SOON THE WHOLE COUNTRYSIDE IS ABLAZE WITH THESE GLORIOUS EMBLEMS OF EASTER.

ITS LIFES PURPOSE ACCOMPLISHED IN THIS BRIEF SPELL, THE CENTURY PLANT DIES, LEAVING NOTHING BUT A HOLLOW PULPY 20 FOOT POLE TO MARK THE SITE OF ITS DRAB LIFE AND FINAL BLAZE OF GLORY

BUT THIS IS NOT QUITE THE END OF THE STORY. THE HOLLOW DAGGER POLES. ARE LIGHT AS FEATHERS, SMALL BOYS CUT THEM DOWN AND BIND THEM TOGETHER INTO RAFTS (THEY ARE TOO FLIMSY TO TAKE A NAIL), WE CALL THEM DAGGER BOATS, AND MANY A WEST INDIAN SAILOR HAS DERIVED HIS FIRST EXPERIENCE OF SHIP CONSTRUCTION, SEAMANSHIP AND OWNERSHIP IN HIS OWN DAGGER BOAT

JELLY NUTS

BEFORE THE COCONUT RIPENS, THE OUTSIDE HUSK IS GREEN AND INSIDE THE SHELL, THE KERNEL IS A SOFT TRANSPARENT JELLY AND THE "MILK" IS A CLEAR, ALMOST TASTELESS, LIQUID

THEY ARE THEN CALLED JELLY NUTS, AND THIS IS HOW WE LIKE THEM HERE. BUT YOU HAVE TO CLIMB THE TREE TO GET THEM — OR RATHER SOME SMALL BOY HAS TO.

THE TOP OF THE HUSK IS THEN CUT OFF AND A HOLE PIERCED IN THE SHELL WITH AN INSTRUMENT WHICH WE CALL A CUTLASS, AND YOU CALL A MACHETE. THIS IS ALSO BEST LEFT TO THE SMALL BOY.

THE JELLY NUT IS THEN READY TO DRINK. BUT SOME PEOPLE ADD GIN OR RUM FOR OBSCURE REASONS OF THEIR OWN.

WHEN THE NUT RIPENS, IT FALLS TO THE GROUND. THE OUTSIDE HUSK IS THEN GOLDEN BROWN. INSIDE THE SHELL THE KERNEL IS HARD AND WHITE AND THE "MILK" IS CLOUDY AND HAS A PUNGENT COCONUT FLAVOUR WHICH NOBODY DRINKS HERE.

THEY ARE THEN CALLED DRY NUTS

DRY NUTS HAVE THEIR USES. THE HUSKS MAKE COCONUT MATTING, COIR ROPE ETC. THE SHELLS CAN BE USED FOR FUEL. THE KERNELS ARE EXTRACTED AND DRIED IN THE SUN TO MAKE COPRA. OR THE WHOLE NUT (WITHOUT ITS HUSK) CAN BE EXPORTED FOR SALE IN SUPERMARKETS.

COPRA GOES TO THE OIL FACTORY WHERE IT IS CRUSHED TO EXTRACT THE OIL. WHAT REMAINS IS SOLD AS CATTLE FEED.

THE COCONUT OIL CAN BE USED, AS IS, FOR SUNTAN LOTION. BUT IT SMELLS. WHEN THE SMELL HAS BEEN ELIMINATED, THE COCONUT OIL IS BROKEN DOWN CHEMICALLY INTO FAT (WHICH IS USED TO MAKE SOAP) AND COOKING OIL.

THIS COOKING OIL, AS IS, HAS NO COLOUR. SO IT IS DYED YELLOW TO SUIT THE HOUSEWIFE.

13

DON'T STOCK UP WITH STAMPS TO LAST OUT THE CRUISE.
THE STAMPS YOU BUY HERE CAN ONLY BE USED IN THIS ISLAND.
EACH ISLAND HAS ITS OWN STAMPS

IN FACT, EACH ISLAND IS A SEPARATE POLITICAL ENTITY.
EACH BRITISH ISLAND IS LINKED TO THE CROWN.

QUEEN ELIZABETH IS QUEEN OF MONTSERRAT AND QUEEN OF St LUCIA
(AS WELL AS BEING QUEEN OF CANADA AND ONE OR TWO OTHER PLACES)

BUT THERE IS NO LINK AT ALL BETWEEN THE ISLANDS THEMSELVES.
FEDERATION WAS ORGANISED IN 1963, BUT DID NOT "TAKE"
CONSEQUENTLY EACH ISLAND HAS :—

   ITS OWN GOVERNMENT
   ITS OWN LAWS
   ITS OWN TAXES

(THIS WILL NOT SOUND ODD TO AMERICANS SINCE THE SAME CAN BE
SAID OF THEIR STATES EVEN AFTER 200 YEARS OF FEDERATION)

—

THE FRENCH ISLANDS, MARTINIQUE AND GUADELOUPE,
ARE BOTH DÉPARTEMENTS OF FRANCE. A DÉPARTEMENT IS
THE EQUIVALENT OF A STATE IN THE U.S.A.
SO, THE STATUS OF THESE FRENCH ISLANDS IS THE SAME AS
THAT OF ALASKA AND HAWAII.

—

THE AMERICAN AND DUTCH ISLANDS HAVE A DIFFERENT
STATUS AGAIN IN RELATION TO THEIR MOTHER COUNTRIES.

14

CURRENCY

THE FOLLOWING CURRENCIES ARE IN USE HERE :—

IN THE BRITISH ISLANDS $ BWI ($5 U.S. = $10 BWI IN 1968)
  "   "   FRENCH   "   FRENCH FRANCS ($1 U.S. = 5 N.F. IN 1968)
  "   "   DUTCH   "   ANY CURRENCY

YOU CAN GET BY WITH U.S DOLLAR NOTES ALMOST ANYWHERE.
BUT NOBODY WILL TAKE U.S. (OR OTHER FOREIGN) COINS.

THE FRENCH ISLANDS WILL NOT TAKE $ BWI.
  "   BRITISH   "   "   "   " FRENCH FRANCS.

BE CAREFUL IN GRENADA, WHERE THEY USE AN OBSOLETE BWI CURRENCY
WHICH IS NO LONGER CURRENT ELSEWHERE.

TRINIDAD HAS ITS OWN NOTES, EQUAL IN VALUE TO $ BWI, BUT NOT CURRENT
ELSEWHERE. BARBADOS WILL SOON HAVE THEIR OWN TOO.

TRAVELLERS CHEQUES CAN BE CASHED IN ANY BANK, AND SOMETIMES
CAN BE USED AS CURRENCY ALONG THE TOURIST ROUTE.
BUT WE TRY TO KEEP OFF THE TOURIST
ROUTE, SO DO PLEASE KEEP SOME
LOCAL CURRENCY.

DINER'S CLUB CARD
OR TRAVELLERS
CHEQUE ?

THE "FORMALITIES"

CUSTOMS   HEALTH   IMMIGRATION   HARBOUR M.

As each island is a separate country, the international rules for entry and clearance of shipping (which includes yachts) apply. When given the full works (which happens in U.S ports) it can be hell. Here, they reduce it all to a mere formality.

It is my job as skipper to ensure that the required formalities are attended to with as little inconvenience as possible to you.

Actually they affect you very little except that:—
- (a) We must make our first call in any island at a "Port of Entry" when you might have preferred somewhere else
- (b) The formalities sometimes suffer from delays.

Your own papers will not be called for until you finally disembark.

If you should think, as I do, that even these formalities are troublesome, irrelevant to tourism and unnecessary, the right point of attack is in Washington or London. As long as the big countries continue to harry their tourists, the smaller countries will follow suit.

Q FLAG (yellow flag) is the international single letter code meaning
"My ship is healthy. I require free practique"
It is always hoisted when first entering from abroad.

SMUGGLING

AMONG WEST INDIANS THE
WORD SMUGGLER RETAINS
SOME OF THE GLAMOUROUS
OVERTONES WHICH ARE ALSO
ASSOCIATED WITH THE WORD
BUCCANEER.

SMUGGLING IS SO WIDESPREAD THAT IT MIGHT ALMOST BE
CLASSIFIED AS A COTTAGE INDUSTRY.

THEY CALL IT "DE GAME" AND THEY PLAY IT WITH THE SAME GAY ABANDON
THAT THEY ADOPT IN CRICKET. THEY OFTEN GET THEIR SLOOPS
IMPOUNDED BY THE AUTHORITIES AS A RESULT.

NONE OF THIS, OF COURSE, HAS ANYTHING TO DO WITH YACHTS.

NO YACHTSMAN WOULD BE SO FOOLISH AS TO RISK HIS EXPENSIVE VESSEL
FOR THE SAKE OF THE PALTRY FEW DOLLARS WHICH HE MIGHT MAKE
OUT OF SMUGGLING. IT WOULD MAKE NO SENSE AT ALL

BUT THE AUTHORITIES, SUSPECTING SMUGGLERS EVERYWHERE, CANNOT
BELIEVE THAT THE YACHTS DO NOT SMUGGLE, AND CANNOT UNDERSTAND
WHY THEY DON'T.

SO WE ARE IN THE DIFFICULT POSITION OF HAVING TO BE,
NOT ONLY FREE FROM FAULT, BUT ALSO ABOVE SUSPICION.

THREE IMAGINARY PERILS

OF THE TROPICS

1. ### THE BARRACUDA IS A SAVAGE

LOOKING CREATURE WHICH STRIKES
TERROR INTO THE HUMAN HEART WITH
ITS BALEFUL EYE AND GNASHING TEETH.

BUT RECORDS DATING BACK 300 YEARS
CAN ONLY AUTHENTICATE 19 NIPS
ON HUMAN BEINGS.

AS A PLAYTHING, HE IS MUCH
LESS DANGEROUS THAN THE
AVERAGE PUPPY.

2. ### THE SHARK.

THERE ARE SOME SHARKS IN THE
WEST INDIES, BUT NOTHING APPROACHING
THE SHARK DENSITY IN LONG ISLAND SOUND.

SHARKS ARE KNOWN TO HAVE ATTACKED
HUMAN BEINGS IN SOME PARTS OF THE WORLD,
BUT NOT IN THE WEST INDIES. PERHAPS WE
HAVE THE WRONG SORT.

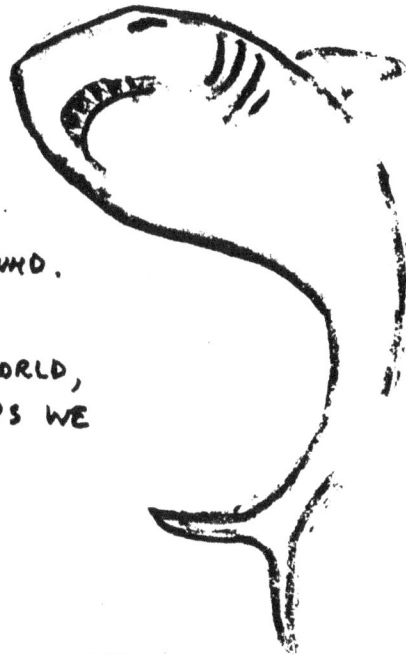

3. ### SNAKES. THE FER DE LANCE IN

MARTINIQUE IS VERY POISONOUS, BUT
THE CHANCES OF YOUR MEETING ONE
ARE ABOUT THE SAME AS OF MEETING
A BEAR IN 5TH AVENUE (THERE ARE
PLENTY OF BEARS IN NEW YORK STATE)

I DO NOT SAY THAT THESE THINGS ARE
NOT FRIGHTENING, I SIMPLY SAY THAT
THEY ARE NOT DANGEROUS — WHICH IS
QUITE A DIFFERENT THING.

I ALSO BELIEVE THAT OBSESSION WITH
THESE IMAGINARY PERILS DISTRACTS ATTENTION
WHICH SHOULD BE GIVEN TO THE REAL PERILS (DESCRIBED ELSEWHERE

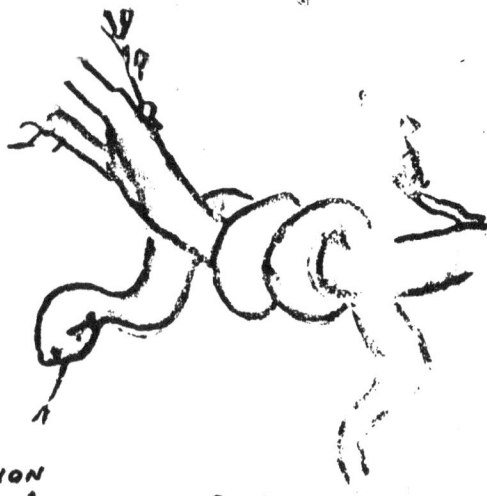

THE THREE REAL PERILS
OF THE TROPICS

1. <u>THE SUN</u> , BY FAR THE MOST PERILOUS OF THE THREE BECAUSE PEOPLE WILL INSIST ON USING METHODS SUITABLE FOR TEMPERATE CLIMATES (AND THIS INCLUDES FLORIDA) AND WILL LIE OUT IN THE SUN.

HERE, YOU WILL GET ALL YOU NEED, AND RETURN HOME WITH AN ENVIABLE TAN, BY JUST STAYING UNDER THE AWNINGS. BY LYING OUT IN THE SUN, YOU WILL GET SUN-POISONING WHICH HAS SPOILT SO MANY YACHTING HOLIDAYS HERE, AND YOU WILL RETURN HOME BLOTCHED AND PEELING.

USE SUN-TAN OILS BY ALL MEANS, BUT DON'T RELY ON THEM. OTHERWISE YOU WILL BE YET ANOTHER SUN CASUALTY.

2. <u>MANCHINEEL APPLES</u>   DON'T EAT ANY SMALL GREEN APPLES WHICH YOU WILL SEE LYING AROUND IN PROFUSION. THEY ARE HIGHLY POISONOUS. THE MANCHINEEL TREE ALSO HAS A POOR REPUTATION DUE TO ITS POISONOUS FRUIT. I HAVE NEVER SEEN THIS JUSTIFIED. BUT JUST IN CASE...

3. <u>BLACK SEA URCHINS</u>   HAVE LONG, SHARP, BRITTLE, BARBED SPIKES WHICH PIERCE THE SKIN AND THEN BREAK OFF. THEY ARE THEN PRACTICALLY IMPOSSIBLE TO DIG OUT   THEY GROW MOSTLY ON CORAL AND ROCKS, BUT SOMETIMES ON SANDY BEACHES, WHERE THEY ARE EASY TO SEE, PARTICULARLY WHEN WEARING GOGGLES. WITH NORMAL CARE, THEY ARE EASY TO AVOID, BUT IT IS SURPRISING HOW MANY PEOPLE BUMP INTO THEM.   SO, TAKE CARE. THEY ARE VERY COMMON AND VERY UNCOMFORTABLE.

LANGUAGES

ALONG THE "TOURIST ROUTE", MOST PEOPLE SPEAK ENGLISH. NO PROBLEM.
BUT WE LIKE TO GET AWAY FROM THE TOURIST ROUTE, AND THE FOLLOWING
REMARKS APPLY THERE.

IN THE FRENCH ISLANDS THE OFFICIAL LANGUAGE IS FRENCH. MOST
PEOPLE SPEAK IT AND THEY WILL DO SO TO YOU AND ME.
BETWEEN THEMSELVES, THEY SPEAK A FRENCH PATOIS,
WHICH EVEN A FRENCHMAN CANNOT UNDERSTAND.
YOU WILL HEAR THIS ALL THE TIME, BUT THERE IS
LITTLE POINT IN TRYING TO UNDERSTAND IT.

IN THE BRITISH ISLANDS THE OFFICIAL
LANGUAGE IS ENGLISH, AND MOST PEOPLE
SPEAK IT.
IN DOMINICA, ST LUCIA & GRENADA,
THEY SPEAK A FRENCH PATOIS.
IN THE OTHER ISLANDS, THE DIALECT
MAY BE HARD TO FOLLOW, BUT IT IS
BASICALLY ENGLISH AND NOT A PATOIS.

IN THE DUTCH ISLANDS, HARDLY ANYONE SPEAKS DUTCH.

A FEW PITFALLS

IN THE FRENCH ISLANDS, A RUM PUNCH MEANS SOMETHING QUITE
DIFFERENT FROM WHAT YOU MEAN. IF YOU ORDER A MARTINI, IT WILL
PROBABLY COME OUT OF A BOTTLE LABELLED "MARTINI" AND NOT, AS
YOU MAY EXPECT, OUT OF A BOTTLE LABELLED "GIN".
TRY TO DISTINGUISH BETWEEN THE PRONUNCIATION OF "BIERRE",
WHICH IS WHAT YOU WANT, AND "BYRRH", WHICH YOU DON'T.

CREOLE

THE WORD ORIGINALLY, DESIGNATED THE PEOPLE OF WHITE FAMILIES PERMANENTLY
RESIDENT IN THE WEST INDIES. IT WAS A "STATUS WORD" AND THE
PHRASE "RICH AS A CREOLE" WAS CURRENT IN EUROPE.
NOW IT MEANS ABOUT AS MANY DIFFERENT THINGS AS THERE ARE
PEOPLE WHO USE THE WORD. BUT TAKE CARE ABOUT USING IT IN ITS
ORIGINAL SENSE. YOU MIGHT GIVE MORTAL OFFENCE.

LOBSTERS

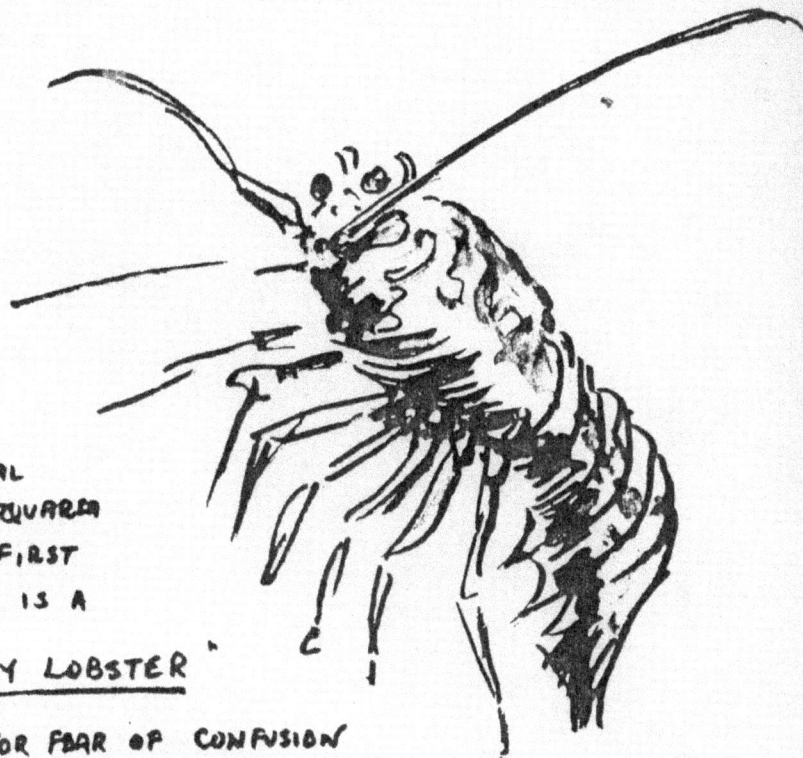

OFFICIALLY,
THAT IS TO SAY IN
TEXTBOOKS, NATURAL
HISTORY MUSEUMS, AQUARIA
ETc., THIS CHAP'S FIRST
AND OFFICIAL NAME IS A

"SPINY LOBSTER"

MOST AMERICANS, FOR FEAR OF CONFUSION
WITH THE PRECIOUS MAINE LOBSTERS, WILL
GIVE HIM HIS SECOND TITLE "CRAYFISH OR CRAWFISH" WHICH HE
SHARES WITH A LARGE NUMBER OF OTHER CRUSTACEANS, MANY OF
THEM FRESH WATER SPECIES.

THE FRENCH CALL HIM "LANGOUSTE" AND HAVE OTHER
NAMES FOR THE OTHER SPECIES OF CRAYFISH (LANGOUSTINE, ECRIVISSE
THEY HAVE AN ENTIRELY DIFFERENT NAME, "HOMARD" FOR THE
MAINE VARIETY WHICH FLOURISH (DARE I SAY IT) IN THE ENGLISH
CHANNEL TOO.

HE DOES NOT LIVE IN ENGLISH WATERS (TOO COLD)
SO THE ENGLISH MERELY COPY OTHER PEOPLE'S NAMES FOR HIM. USUALLY
"LANGOUSTE." THE NAME LOBSTER, IN ENGLAND MEANS THE SAME
AS IT DOES IN MAINE.

THE ITALIANS, WHO HAVE NO COLD WATER SEAS AND HENCE
NO MAINE TYPE LOBSTERS, BUT PLENTY OF OUR FRIEND ABOVE, CALL
THE WHOLE LOT "ARRAGOSTA".

THE WEST INDIANS, WHO HAVE NO COLD WATER SEAS
EITHER, CALL HIM A "LOBSTER", WHICH GOES RIGHT BACK TO HIS
OFFICIAL NAME. THEY ALSO HAVE SOME FRESH WATER CRUSTACEANS
WHICH THEY CALL CRAYFISH.

CONCLUSION DON'T BE TOO SUBTLE ABOUT ALL THIS. JUST CALL THEM
LOBSTERS AND THE BOYS WILL UNDERSTAND.

"ARE THEY DOLPHINS OR PORPOISES?"

(IF YOU HAVE NO DOUBT ABOUT THE ANSWER, SKIP THIS PAGE. IT WILL ONLY CREATE CONFUSION)

THE FAMILY OF DELPHINIDAE (DOLPHINS IN ENGLISH) IS LARGE. SOME SPECIES IN IT ARE BIGGER THAN SOME SPECIES IN THEIR COUSIN FAMILY, THE WHALES. OTHERS ARE SMALLER.

BUT ALL ARE MAMMALS, WITH BONE STRUCTURES SIMILAR TO OUR OWN. THEY BREATHE AIR. THEY GIVE BIRTH TO, AND FEED THEIR YOUNG LIKE ANY OTHER MAMMAL.

IN SOME ENGLISH SPEAKING COUNTRIES, CERTAIN OF THE SMALLER SPECIES OF DOLPHINS ARE POPULARLY KNOWN AS PORPOISES. UNFORTUNATELY THIS POPULAR NAME IS USED IN DIFFERENT COUNTRIES TO DESCRIBE DIFFERENT SPECIES OF DOLPHINS.

SO THERE IS NO CORRECT ANSWER TO THE QUESTION WITHOUT SPECIFYING AMERICAN, ENGLISH OR AUSTRALIAN USAGE. ETC.

AT THIS POINT ONE MIGHT BE TEMPTED TO CALL THEM ALL DOLPHINS AND BE DONE WITH IT. (AND INCIDENTELLY BE CORRECT).

BUT AGAIN UNFORTUNATELY THERE IS A FURTHER CONFUSION (IN THE ENGLISH LANGUAGE ONLY) AS THERE IS A FISH WHICH HAS ALSO BEEN GIVEN THE NAME OF DOLPHIN. A VERY GOOD EATING FISH TOO

NEEDLESS TO SAY, THERE IS NO CONNECTION WHATEVER BETWEEN THESE TWO CREATURES ANY MORE THAN THERE IS BETWEEN A CATFISH AND A CAT. BUT THE POSSIBILITY THAT SOMEBODY, BEING GIVEN DOLPHIN FOR DINNER, MIGHT THINK THAT HE WAS BEING ASKED TO EAT ONE OF THOSE CHARMING LITTLE CREATURES WHICH GAMBOL ROUND THE BOWS IS SO HORRIFYING THAT I PERSONALLY CALL ALL MAMMAL DOLPHINS PORPOISES — CORRECT OR NOT.

"WHAT'S IT LIKE ?
IS IT COLD ? "

THIS INVARIABLE REMARK, REPEATED A THOUSAND TIMES IN MY HEARING, IS NOT REALLY A QUESTION, BUT RATHER A CONDITIONED REFLEX, BROUGHT ON BY YEARS OF "SHIVERING ON THE BRINK" IN, WHAT IS KNOWN AS THE "TEMPERATE" ZONE. THE SEA WATER TEMPERATURE HERE VARIES ONLY 2° OR 3°, AND COULD NEVER BE DESCRIBED AS COLD, IF WORDS MEAN ANYTHING AT ALL. AND THE SPEAKER KNOWS THIS PERFECTLY WELL, BUT THE REFLEX PREVAILS.

ANOTHER COLLECTOR'S PIECE IS THE REMARK "I NEVER SWIM UNTIL THE TEMPERATURE IS OVER 80°". ANYONE WHO HAS LIVED IN COUNTRIES WHERE THE BATHING WATER IS OVER 80° WILL INSTANTLY REALISE THAT THE SPEAKER HAS NOT DONE SO. AS HE PROBABLY MEANS SOMETHING, IT MOST LIKELY IS "I JUST DON'T WANT TO SWIM". BUT THIS SOUNDS LESS SOPHISTICATED.

TIDES AND CURRENTS

As everyone knows, tides are caused
by the attraction of the moon on the ocean.
This takes the form of two very long,
very low waves which travel round
the earth each day.

In midocean, the rise and fall
caused by these waves is seldom
more than one or two feet. But
they pile up when they meet a large
land mass, and we call that a big rise
and fall of tide. When they run up estuaries,
these waves get bigger still and result in a very high rise and fall of
tide (cf. Bay of Fundy or St Malo Bay with a 40 foot rise and fall)

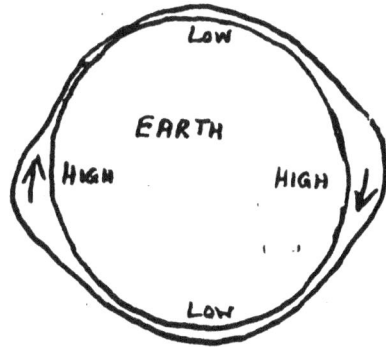

Here, we are in an oceanic area and so get very little rise and
fall of tide and very little tidal current.

The only place where you are likely to notice any current is
when swimming in the Grenadines. When the tidal current is
flowing to the east it will cancel out a permanent ocean current
flowing to the west and the resultant current will be nil.
When the tidal current is flowing to the west it will add to the ocean
current, and the combined current is faster than you can swim.

So, look before you plunge. Better still, follow the
universal safety rule, which applies all over the world
whenever swimming from a boat
at anchor ... always

"SWIM TOWARDS THE BOW"

NOTE. (FOR ADVANCED STUDENTS ONLY)

In oceanic areas the tidal
current flows :-

Towards the moon when the
moon is above the horizon.

Away from the moon when the
moon is below the horizon.

"IS SHE BIG ENOUGH TO CROSS THE ATLANTIC?"

IN THE FIRST PLACE, THE SIZE OF A SHIP DOES NOT GOVERN HER SAFETY AT SEA, ALTHOUGH IT MAY AFFECT HER COMFORT.

SMALL SHIPS ARE AFFECTED BY SMALL WAVES, AND BIG SHIPS ARE AFFECTED BY BIG WAVES, WHICH OFTEN LEAVE THE SMALL SHIP GENTLY BOBBING UP AND DOWN. THE BIG WAVE WHICH SMASHED THE BRIDGE OF THE ITALIAN LINER MICHAELANGELO WOULD PROBABLY NOT HAVE BEEN NOTICED IN A SMALL SHIP.

THE SIZE OF LONG DISTANCE CRUISING YACHTS IS GOVERNED BY OTHER FACTORS - MAINLY CREW.

A LARGE YACHT NEEDS A LARGE CREW. IF THESE ARE PROFESSIONAL, THE OWNER MUST BE VERY RICH, AND NOONE AS RICH AS THIS CAN AFFORD THE TIME FOR REALLY LONG DISTANCE CRUISING. NO MILLIONNAIRE HAS EVER YET SAILED ROUND THE WORLD.

SO THE LARGE CREW MUST BE AMATEUR, AND EXPERIENCE HAS SHOWN THAT THIS JUST DOES NOT WORK.. MANY HAVE STARTED, BUT FEW FINISH.

WHAT THEN IS THE IDEAL NUMBER IN CREW?

PERHAPS THREE.? THEN TWO GANG UP AGAINST ONE, AND THAT FAILS.

PERHAPS TWO? BUT THEN, AS ONE CELEBRATED WORLD CRUISING YACHTSMAN ONCE REMARKED "IF YOU WANT TO KEEP YOUR CREW FOR A LONG JOURNEY, YOU WILL HAVE TO MARRY HER".

SO PERHAPS THIS IS THE REASON WHY MOST "WORLD GIRDLERS" ARE MARRIED COUPLES, AND WHY SINGLE-HANDERS RUN THEM CLOSE.

THE FACT REMAINS THAT NEARLY ALL LONG DISTANCE CRUISING YACHTS ARE SMALL.

"IS IT ALWAYS AS ROUGH AS THIS HERE?"

THE SHORT ANSWER TO THIS IS PROBABLY "YES", AS CONDITIONS IN THE TRADE WIND BELT ARE PRETTY CONSTANT THROUGHOUT THE YEAR. BUT A MORE INSTRUCTIVE ANSWER BRINGS IN THE QUESTION OF WHICH WAY THE SHIP IS GOING.

WITH TWO IDENTICAL VESSELS IN THE SAME SPOT, ONE CAN BE HAVING ROUGH WEATHER AND THE OTHER CALM.

FOR A SAILING BOAT, THE CALMEST RIDE IS USUALLY WITH THE WIND ABEAM, WHICH IS LUCKY BECAUSE WE GET MORE BEAM WINDS BETWEEN OUR ISLANDS THAN ANY OTHER. FOR A MOTOR BOAT, A BEAM WIND IS ABOUT THE WORST, AND THAT IS WHY WE HAVE FEW MOTOR BOATS HERE AMONG THE CRUISING YACHTS.

SWELLS IN HARBOUR

MOST OF OUR HARBOURS ARE OPEN ANCHORAGES WHICH ARE WELL PROTECTED FROM THE EASTERLY SWELLS CREATED BY THE TRADE WIND, WHICH IS PRACTICALLY THE ONLY WIND WE GET.

BUT SWELLS CREATED BY STORMS ELSEWHERE CAN TRAVEL INCREDIBLY LONG DISTANCES IN CALM WATER, AND THESE MAY COME FROM ANY DIRECTION AND DISTURB OUR OPEN ANCHORAGES.

SO WE GET THIS APPARENT PARADOX :—

IF A STRONG WIND IS BLOWING IT WILL KILL ANY SWELL COMING FROM OTHER DIRECTIONS, AND OUR OPEN ANCHORAGES WILL BE CALM. IF THE WIND IS LIGHT, SWELLS COMING FROM OUTSIDE OUR AREA MAY PENETRATE INTO OUR OPEN ANCHORAGES AND DISTURB THEM.

CHECK-OFF LIST FOR A QUICK DIP
ON A SANDY BEACH

"JUST A QUICK DIP. BUT WE HAD BETTER TAKE A FEW THINGS ALONG...

MASKS, SCHNORKELS AND FLIPPERS. TWO SPEARGUNS WILL BE ENOUGH.
BATHING CAPS. TOWELS FOR SIX. SHORTS AND SPORTS SHIRTS.
DON'T FORGET THE SUN-TAN LOTION — AND SOME ANTI-BUG SPRAY.
SWEATERS IN CASE IT IS COLD, DON'T YOU THINK. ALSO HATS AND SNEAKERS
MOVIE AND STILL CAMERAS, AND WE'D BEST TAKE SOME SPARE FILMS.
SUN GLASSES, BOOKS, MAGAZINES, WRITING PAPER, PENS AND READING
GLASSES. BETTER TAKE SOME B.W.I. LIGHT RAINCOATS IN CASE OF SHOWERS.
CIGARETTES, LIGHTERS (BETTER REFILL THEM FIRST) HOW ABOUT A THERMOS
WITH SOMETHING COLD IN IT. AND A FEW CRACKERS TO NIBBLE (NOTHING
ELABORATE, RENNIE, WE WILL ONLY BE ASHORE A FEW MINUTES) WE'D BETTER
TAKE THE RADIO, AND HOW ABOUT THE WALKIE-TALKIE IN CASE WE HAVE
FORGOTTEN ANYTHING. OH! AND HAVE YOU GOT AN OLD SAIL TO USE AS
AN AWNING? WE ARE ALMOST READY NOW, SKIPPER.
WHAT! COCKTAIL TIME ALREADY?
LETS FORGET THE WHOLE THING AND GO FOR A SWIM
OVER THE SHIPS SIDE INSTEAD. "

FREELANCE

"THE CHILDREN ARE ALL GREAT
SAILORS, CAPTAIN.
YOUR CREW WILL HARDLY NEED TO
DO A THING".

"IS SHE A SHIP OR IS SHE A BOAT?"

ALTHOUGH THERE IS SOME CONNOTATION OF SIZE BETWEEN THE WORDS "SHIP" AND "BOAT" IN THE NAUTICAL LANGUAGE, THERE IS NO CLEAR DIVIDING MARK. WHOEVER DEVISED THE IDEA THAT "A BOAT IS SOMETHING THAT YOU CAN HOIST INTO A SHIP" DID NOT SPEAK THE NAUTICAL LANGUAGE.

MUCH MORE COMMONLY, THE TWO WORDS ARE USED IN CONNECTION WITH DIFFERENT ASPECTS OF A VESSEL. CONSIDER THE FOLLOWING PHRASES :—

1/ SS QUEEN MARY IS A GOOD SEA BOAT, BUT JUST TRY ASKING HER CAPTAIN WHEN HIS BOAT SAILS.

A GOOD SEA BOAT

2/ SUBMARINES ARE ALWAYS KNOWN AS BOATS, BUT THEY HAVE SHIPS COMPANIES, SHIPS OFFICES ETC.

3/ VESSELS OF WHATEVER SIZE HAVE SHIPS PAPERS AND EMBARK SHIPS STORES.

4/ FERRY BOATS (NOT FERRY SHIPS) COME IN ALMOST ALL SIZES

IF YOU CAN DETECT A LOGICAL PATTERN IN THIS YOU ARE A GENIUS. BUT DON'T EXPECT ANYTHING TOO LOGICAL OUT OF THE NAUTICAL LANGUAGE IN WHICH MODERN OCEAN LINERS STILL "SAIL".

"SHIPS PAPERS PLEASE"

IF YOU STILL WANT AN ANSWER TO YOUR QUESTION, WILL YOU PLEASE FIRST ANSWER THESE TWO :—

"IS THAT YOUR HOUSE OR IS IT YOUR HOME?"

"IS HE A LAWYER OR IS HE YOUR HUSBAND?"

"DO YOU CHARTER OUT OF ANTIGUA?"

A SIMPLE STRAIGHTFORWARD QUESTION WHICH DESERVES A SIMPLE REPLY. BUT....

WHEN YOU CHARTER "OUT OF NASSAU", YOU JOIN THE SHIP AT NASSAU AND YOU RETURN TO NASSAU AT THE END OF THE CHARTER.

THE SAME CAN BE SAID OF MIAMI, CANNES, ST THOMAS AND ALMOST ANYWHERE ELSE.

BUT HERE, THIS IS NOT SO.

YOU MAY JOIN THE SHIP AT ANY PLACE IN THE ISLAND CHAIN AND RETURN TO ANY OTHER, AT THE END OF THE CHARTER. IT IS MOST UNUSUAL TO START AND FINISH AT THE SAME ISLAND WHICH WOULD INVOLVE BACK-TRACKING) AND ANTIGUA IS ONLY ONE OF A DOZEN STARTING AND FINISHING PLACES.

SO WHAT IS THE SIMPLE STRAIGHTFORWARD ANSWER TO THIS SIMPLE QUESTION?

"IS THIS ONE OF NICHOLSON'S YACHTS?"

THE SIMPLE REPLY "YES" IS NOT ONLY INCORRECT BUT ALSO IMPLIES A PURELY CHARTER BOAT STATUS, WHICH ALSO IS SOMETHING LESS THAN THE TRUTH. AT THE OPPOSITE EXTREME, ONE FINE YACHT, OWNED BY AN INTERNATIONALLY FAMOUS FAMILY, USED TO ADOPT THE FOLLOWING DIGNIFIED GAMBIT :-
"NO. THE OWNER DOES NOT CHARTER. BUT HE LENDS THE YACHT TO PARTIES OF HIS FRIENDS FROM TIME TO TIME."
THIS IS GOING TOO FAR. (THE YACHT HAS NOW BEEN SOLD).

THE BEST ANSWER IS "YES. WE CHARTER THROUGH NICHOLSON'S AGENCY."
THIS MAKES IT CLEAR THAT THE SHIP IS AVAILABLE FOR CHARTER, AND MAY LEAVE THE QUESTIONER WITH A VAGUE, AND POSSIBLY ALLURING, IMPRESSION THAT THERE IS SOMETHING ELSE IN THE BACKGROUND. AND, OF COURSE, THERE IS!

OUR SEASONS

THE FOLLOWING ARE NON-SEASONAL HERE:-

1/ THE WEATHER, WHICH IS REMARKABLY STABLE IN THE TRADE WIND BELT. SUCH VARIATIONS AS THERE ARE IN WIND, TEMPERATURE AND RAIN, ARE MORE MARKED FROM ONE WEEK TO ANOTHER THAN THEY ARE BETWEEN ONE SEASON AND THE NEXT.

2/ BANANAS & COCONUTS RIPEN THROUGHOUT THE YEAR.

THE FOLLOWING ARE SEASONAL HERE: —

3/ FLOWERING TREES AND SHRUBS WHICH FLOURISH IN THE SUMMER BEGINNING WITH THE CENTURY PLANT (OR MAY POLE) IN MAY, AND REACHING ITS CLIMAX WITH THE SPECTACULAR FLAMBOYANT IN JUNE AND JULY.

4/ CITRUS FRUIT (WINTER), MANGOES (SUMMER)

5/ MIGRATORY FISH (SUMMER)

6/ SHORT DAYS AND EARLY SUNSETS (WINTER)

7/ HURRICANES (AUGUST & SEPTEMBER). THESE DISTURB THE NORMAL WEATHER PATTERN HERE IN EXACTLY THE SAME WAY AS THEY DO ON THE EAST COAST OF THE U.S.A, WHICH IS ANOTHER PART OF THE SAME HURRICANE BELT.

8/ TOURISTS. THIS IS THE MOST MARKED SEASONAL PHENOMENON OF THE LOT. BY COMING IN THE WINTER THEY MAY BE CHOOSING THE BEST TIME TO LEAVE HOME, BUT THEY ARE NOT CHOOSING THE BEST SEASON HERE.

MAY POLE.

TRADE WIND ZONES.

THERE ARE TWO TRADE WIND ZONES, ONE NORTH AND ONE SOUTH OF THE EQUATOR, IN WHICH THE WIND BLOWS CONSTANTLY FROM THE EAST. THIS IS DUE TO THE ROTATION OF THE EARTH.

THESE UNCHANGING WINDS CREATE AN UNCHANGING CLIMATE WHICH, LUCKILY FOR US, IS ALSO PRACTICALLY IDEAL. FOR ALL PRACTICAL PURPOSES, IT IS THE SAME, SUMMER OR WINTER, DAY OR NIGHT.

THE TRADE WIND ZONES MOVE NORTH AND SOUTH WITH THE SUN. AND IN CONSEQUENCE MOST AREAS WHICH HAVE A TRADE WIND CLIMATE ONLY HAVE IT FOR A PART OF THE YEAR. BUT THE WINDWARD AND LEEWARD ISLANDS, BEING IN THE MIDDLE OF THE ZONE, ARE NEVER UNCOVERED AND RETAIN ITS BENEVOLENT CLIMATE THROUGHOUT THE YEAR.

THE TRADE WIND CLIMATE IS NOT ENTIRELY UNCHANGING. THE WIND MAY BLOW UP TO 20° ON EITHER SIDE OF EAST AND MAY VARY CORRESPONDINGLY IN STRENGTH. THE WEATHER CAN SOMETIMES BE SHOWERY AND AT OTHER TIMES NOT SO. SUCH CHANGES OCCUR PERIODICALLY THROUGHOUT THE YEAR AND ONE SET OF CONDITIONS WILL USUALLY LAST FOR ABOUT TWO WEEKS ("UNTIL THE NEXT CHANGE OF MOON" THEY SAY HERE). SOME PEOPLE TRY TO FORMULATE THESE CHANGES INTO THE SEASONAL PATTERNS WHICH PREVAIL IN CONTINENTAL CLIMATES, BUT WITHOUT VERY CONVINCING RESULTS.

CONTINENTAL WEATHER

A BIG LAND MASS WILL GET HOT BY DAY AND IN SUMMER AND COLD BY NIGHT AND IN WINTER, WHILE THE SEA TEMPERATURE WILL REMAIN RELATIVELY CONSTANT. AS HOT AIR RISES AND COLD AIR SINKS, ALTERNATE LAND AND SEA BREEZES CAN BE EXPECTED AND THESE WILL GIVE RISE TO CHANGEABLE CONDITIONS WHICH ARE THE EXACT REVERSE OF THOSE WHICH OBTAIN IN THE TRADE WIND ZONES.

BEING IN A MARITIME AREA, FAR FROM ANY BIG LAND MASSES, WE DO NOT GET CONTINENTAL WEATHER IN THE WINDWARD AND LEEWARD ISLANDS (THE WIND DOES NOT NECESSARILY DIE AWAY AT SUNSET AND A RED SKY AT NIGHT HAS LITTLE TO DO WITH TOMORROW'S WEATHER)

BUT THE CONVENTIONAL WEATHER WISDOM OF THE WORLD WAS NURTURED IN CONTINENTAL CLIMATES AND IT IS HARD TO LEARN THAT IT IS NOT UNIVERSALLY APPLICABLE.

RAINFALL

RAIN FALLS FOR TWO REASONS HERE :-

1/ THE WARM, MOIST TRADE WIND
BLOWING ACROSS THE ATLANTIC
IS DEFLECTED UPWARDS BY THE
MOUNTAINOUS ISLANDS. THIS
COOLS THE AIR, WHICH CAN THEN
NO LONGER HOLD ITS MOISTURE.
SO IT FALLS IN THE FORM OF
RAIN. THIS PROCESS GOES ON
MOST OF THE TIME. THE HIGHER
THE ISLAND, THE MORE IT RAINS.
IN OPEN SEA AND ON FLAT ISLANDS
THERE WILL BE NO RAINFALL FROM THIS CAUSE.

2/ SOMETIMES WE HAVE JUST PLAIN SHOWERY WEATHER, AND THE
SHOWERS CAN BE SEEN
UNDER GREAT MUSHROOM-
SHAPED CLOUDS WHICH
ADVANCE, DOWN WIND,
ACROSS THE SEA.

THESE SHOWERS, WHICH ARE
VERY HEAVY AS WELL AS
BEING VERY LOCAL, FALL
ON LAND AND SEA ALIKE,
AND THE FLAT ISLANDS GET
THEM AS MUCH AS ANY OTHER.

SO THE MOUNTAINOUS ISLANDS GET FAIRLY CONSTANT RAINFALL, WHILE
THE FLAT ISLANDS DEPEND ON PERIODS OF SHOWERY WEATHER, AND
MONTHS MAY ELAPSE BETWEEN ONE SHOWERY PERIOD AND THE NEXT.

MOST RAIN HERE FALLS IN THE FORM OF HEAVY SHOWERS WHICH LAST
ONLY A FEW MINUTES. VERY OCCASIONALLY WE GET AN ORDINARY RAINY
DAY, AS AT HOME, BUT PRACTICALLY NEVER TWO SUCH DAYS IN SUCCESSION.

HEAVENLY BODIES

THE STARS MOVE DIFFERENTLY HERE
FROM THE WAY THEY DO AT HOME.
TO UNDERSTAND THIS, CONSIDER TWO
EXTREME EXAMPLES

EXAMPLE 1 AT THE NORTH POLE.
THE POLE STAR, WHICH IS THE HUB OF
THE MOVEMENT, IS DIRECTLY OVERHEAD. THE
STARS REVOLVE ROUND AND ROUND IT, ALWAYS
AT THE SAME ALTITUDE ABOVE THE HORIZON.

POLE STAR

AT THE NORTH POLE

EXAMPLE 2 AT THE EQUATOR.
THE POLE STAR, WHICH IS STILL THE HUB OF
THE MOVEMENT, LIES ON THE NORTHERN
HORIZON. THE STARS, STILL REVOLVING
ROUND IT, RISE ON THE EASTERN HORIZON,
PASS UP AND OVER AND SET ON THE
WESTERN HORIZON.

ON THE
EQUATOR

ANYWHERE ELSE, THE MOVEMENT IS
A COMBINATION OF THESE TWO.
THE NEARER THE POLE, THE MORE
THE MOVEMENT IS "ROUND AND ROUND".
THE NEARER THE EQUATOR, THE
MORE THE MOVEMENT IS "UP AND OVER".

IF YOU ARE WITH ME SO FAR, IT
MIGHT BE WORTH GOING ON. IF NOT,
YOU MIGHT AS WELL GIVE UP AND TAKE
TO SCRABBLE, OR TURN TO ANOTHER PART
OF THIS BOOK.

ANYWHERE
ELSE

END OF LESSON Nº1.

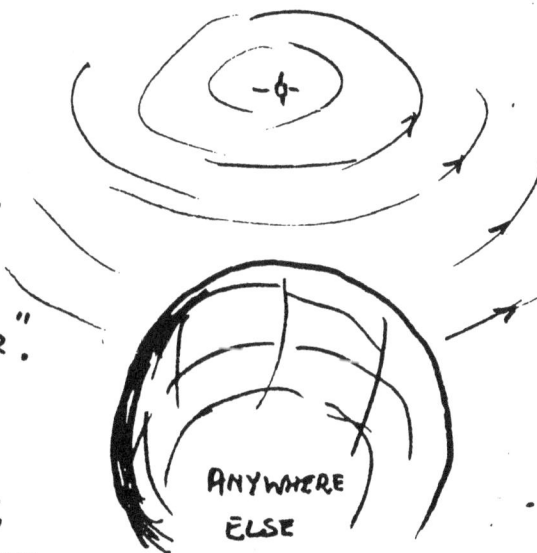

HEAVENLY BODIES (CONTINUED)

AT THE NORTH POLE

1. THE POLAR CONSTELLATIONS (e.g. BIG DIPPER) WILL CIRCLE OVERHEAD.
2. EQUATORIAL CONSTELLATIONS (e.g. ORION) CIRCLE AROUND THE HORIZON.
3. SOUTHERN CONSTELLATIONS (e.g. SOUTHERN CROSS) NEVER APPEAR AT ALL.
   THIS SITUATION NEVER CHANGES.

AT THE EQUATOR, ALL THE STARS IN THE HEAVENS ARE ABOVE THE HORIZON AT SOME PART OF THE 24 HOURS, BUT WHETHER THEY ARE VISIBLE OR NOT DEPENDS ON WHETHER IT IS NIGHT OR DAY.

SO, IN POLAR LATITUDES YOU GET USED TO THE SAME LIMITED ASSORTMENT OF STARS, WHILE IN EQUATORIAL LATITUDES, YOU GET A GREATER VARIETY, AND THE ASSORTMENT CHANGES EVERY DAY.

"CHANGES SLIGHTLY EVERY DAY." (THIS CALLS FOR EXPLANATION)
SINCE THE EARTH REVOLVES AROUND THE SUN ONCE A YEAR, EACH STAR WILL BE IN A DIFFERENT POSITION RELATIVE TO THE SUN EVERY DAY, AND IT WILL NOT BE SURPRISING TO LEARN THAT EACH INDIVIDUAL STAR RISES 4 MINUTES EARLIER EVERY DAY (OR 2 HOURS EARLIER EVERY MONTH OR 24 HOURS EARLIER AFTER ONE YEAR).

EXAMPLE   THE SOUTHERN CROSS

THIS CONSTELLATION RISES :—

IN JANUARY	AT ABOUT	4 A.M.
— FEBRUARY	" "	2 "
— MARCH	" "	MIDNIGHT
— APRIL	" "	10 P.M. (AND SO ON)

SO, WHETHER OR NOT YOU WILL SEE THE SOUTHERN CROSS, AND IF SO AT WHAT TIME OF NIGHT, DEPENDS ON THE MONTH YOU ARE HERE.

THE OTHER GREAT SOUTHERN CONSTELLATIONS OF SCORPIO AND SAGITTARIUS RISE RESPECTIVELY ABOUT TWO AND FOUR HOURS LATER THAN THE SOUTHERN CROSS, AN ARRANGEMENT DESIGNED FOR THE BENEFIT OF SUMMER CHARTERERS.

SCORPIO

END OF LESSON 2   SAGITTARIUS

THE BIG DIPPER

THE BIG DIPPER, LIKE ANY
OTHER CONSTELLATION,
REVOLVES
AROUND THE
POLE STAR ONCE
IN EVERY 24 HOURS.
SOMETIMES IT IS
"ABOVE" THE POLE
STAR AND SOMETIMES
IT IS "BELOW" IT.

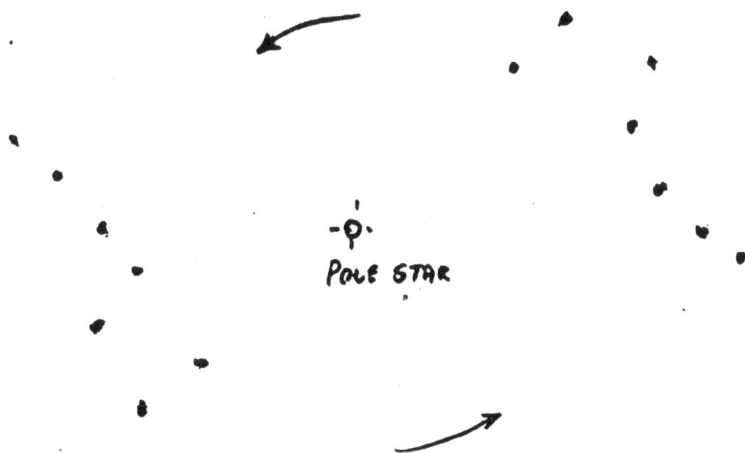

POLE STAR

IN THIS PART OF THE WORLD,
WHERE THE ALTITUDE OF THE POLE STAR ABOVE THE HORISON IS
ONLY 13° (GRENADA) TO 17° (ANTIGUA), THE BIG DIPPER IS BELOW
THE HORISON WHEN IT IS "THE RIGHT WAY UP". WE ONLY SEE IT
HERE WHEN IT IS "UPSIDE DOWN".

FURTHER NORTH,
WHERE THE ALTITUDE OF THE POLE STAR ABOVE THE HORIZON IS
MUCH GREATER (43° IN BOSTON), THE BIG DIPPER IS VISIBLE ON
EITHER SIDE OF THE POLE STAR. WHEN IT IS BELOW THE POLE STAR,
IT IS OBVIOUSLY "THE RIGHT WAY UP". WHEN IT IS ABOVE THE POLE
STAR, ON THE OTHER HAND, IT IS ALMOST DIRECTLY OVERHEAD AND DOES
NOT LOOK EITHER "UPSIDE DOWN" OR "RIGHT WAY UP".

SO DON'T WORRY IF YOU ALWAYS SEE THE BIG DIPPER
UPSIDE DOWN HERE. IT DOES NOT NECESSARILY MEAN THAT IT IS
GOING TO RAIN.

THE POLE STAR CLOCK
THE "POINTERS", OR THE TWO STARS WHICH POINT TOWARDS THE
POLE STAR, CAN BE USED AS A 24-HOUR CLOCK (WORKING ANTI-
CLOCKWISE). THE ONLY THING IS THAT THEY, LIKE ANY OTHER STARS,
CHANGE THEIR POSITION BY 4 MINUTES EVERY DAY (OR TWO HOURS
EVERY MONTH AND 24 HOURS IN THE YEAR). SO YOU HAVE TO KNOW
WHERE TO LOCATE YOUR ZERO, DEPENDING ON THE TIME OF YEAR.

(FOR ADVANCED STUDENTS ONLY.)

TIME OF SUNSET

THE TIME OF SUNSET IN THE TROPICS VARIES MORE
THAN YOU WOULD EXPECT. THE FOLLOWING GRAPH OF
SUNSET IN ANTIGUA IS CALCULATED FROM THE 1967
NAUTICAL ALMANAC.

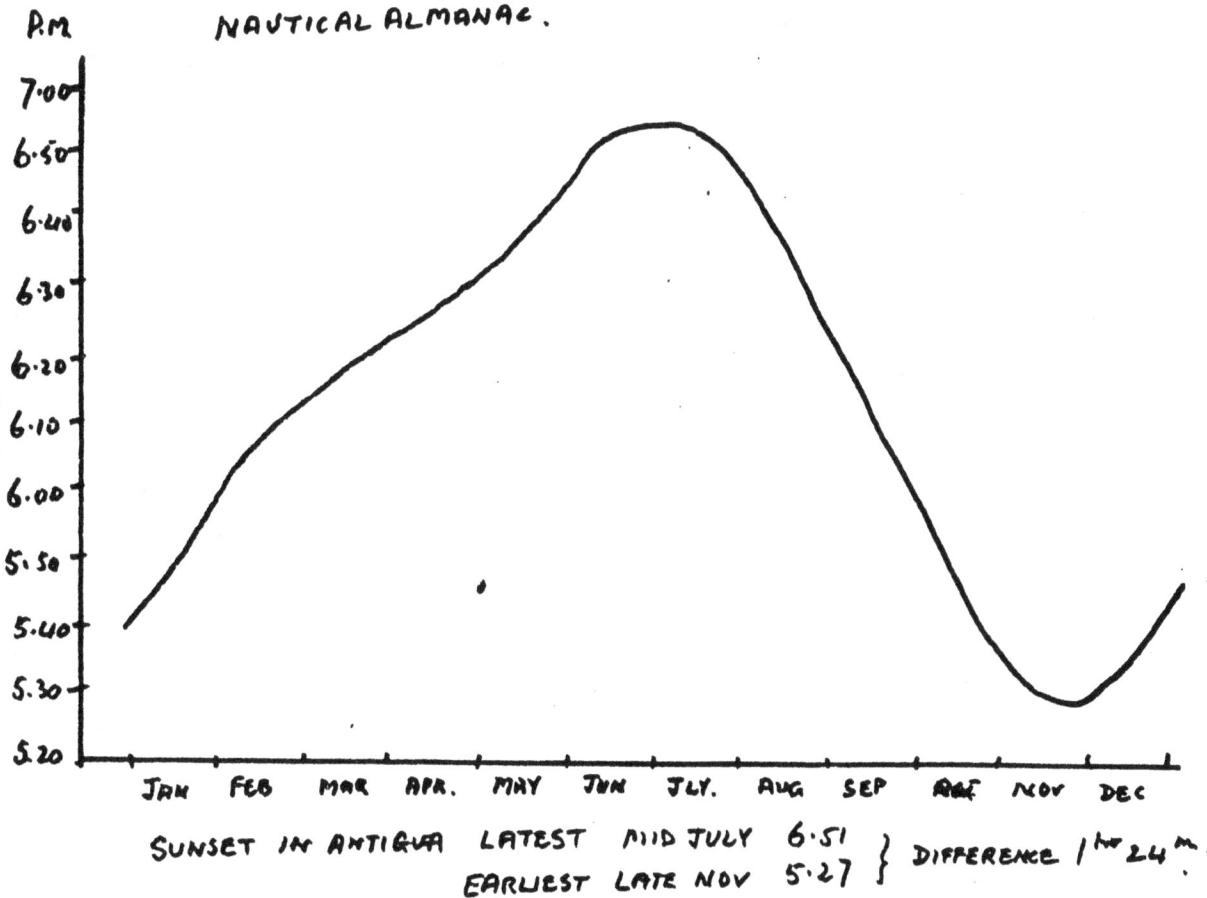

SUNSET IN ANTIGUA   LATEST MID JULY 6.51 } DIFFERENCE 1ʰʳ 24ᵐ
                    EARLIEST LATE NOV 5.27 }

NOTE. (FOR ADVANCED STUDENTS).

IT MAY SEEM ODD THAT THE CURVE IS SO IRREGULAR, THAT ITS
MAXIMUM DOES NOT OCCUR ON THE 21ᵗ JUNE AND THAT ITS
MINIMUM IS NOT ON THE 21ᵗ DECEMBER.

THE BASIC REASON FOR THIS LIES IN THE ELIPTICAL MOVEMENT OF
THE EARTH ROUND THE SUN, IN CONSEQUENCE OF WHICH ALL DAYS
IN THE YEAR ARE OF DIFFERENT LENGTH — SOME MORE THAN 24 HOURS
AND SOME LESS.

SO, AS A MATTER OF PRACTICAL CONVENIENCE, WE REGULATE OUR
CLOCKS, NOT BY THE TRUE SUN (WHICH IS IRREGULAR), BUT BY AN
IMAGINARY SUN, WHICH MEANS THE WHOLE LOT OUT, AND GIVES US A
24 HOUR DAY EVERY DAY.

THE DIFFERENCE BETWEEN THE TRUE SUN (WHICH WE SEE SETTING) AND THE
"MEAN SUN" (BY WHICH WE SET OUR CLOCKS) CAN BE AS MUCH AS 15 MINUTES.
THE SAME EFFECT APPLIES ALL OVER THE WORLD, BUT IN HIGHER LATITUDES
IT IS OVERSHADOWED BY THE MUCH GREATER SEASONAL VARIATION.

37

THE GREEN FLASH

(LE RAYON VERT)

QUITE OFTEN HERE, JUST AS THE LAST THIN SEGMENT OF THE SUN IS DISAPPEARING BELOW THE HORIZON, YOU WILL SEE THE GREEN FLASH.

IT ONLY LASTS A FRACTION OF A SECOND AND YOU MUST KEEP A CAREFUL LOOK OUT.

THE HORIZON MUST BE QUITE CLEAR AND CLOUDLESS AND THE SKY MUST BE RED AND NOT PALE.

REASON. IT HAS NOTHING TO DO WITH THE GREEN SPOTS WHICH CONTINUE IN ONES EYES AFTER LOOKING AT THE RED SUN.

IT IS AN OPTICAL ILLUSION IN THE SAME SENSE AS A RAINBOW IS AN OPTICAL ILLUSION, AND IT DERIVES FROM MUCH THE SAME CAUSES, THE REFRACTION AND ABSORPTION OF DIFFERENT LIGHT FREQUENCIES IN THE DENSE ATMOSPHERE NEAR THE HORIZON.

THERE IS, IN FACT, A RED FLASH WHICH PRECEEDS IT, BUT THIS IS HARDLY DISTINGUISHABLE FROM THE LAST RAYS OF THE SUN ITSELF.

I HAVE ONCE SEEN THE GREEN FLASH AT SUNRISE, BUT TO DO THIS, ONE MUST BE LUCKY TO BE LOOKING AT EXACTLY THE RIGHT SPOT AT THE RIGHT TIME. ALSO, ONE DOESN'T SEE SUNRISES SO OFTEN AS SUNSETS FOR A VARIETY OF REASONS.

THE GREEN FLASH CAN BE PHOTOGRAPHED, BUT THIS REQUIRES BIG EQUIPMENT AND A GREAT DEAL OF SKILL OWING TO THE RAPIDLY CHANGING INTENSITY OF THE LIGHT AT THE MOMENT OF SUNSET.

SEE ALSO THE ARTICLE IN THE "SCIENTIFIC AMERICAN" IF YOU THINK THAT I AM PUTTING A FAST ONE ACROSS.

SHORT TWILIGHT

IN THIS PART OF THE WORLD,
THE SUN RISES AT AMOST 90°
TO THE HORISON, PASSES
MORE OR LESS OVERHEAD,
AND THEN SETS AGAIN ALMOST
AT RIGHT ANGLES TO THE
HORIZON.
IN THIS WAY IT GETS WAY DOWN
BELOW THE HORIZON IN THE
QUICKEST POSSIBLE TIME.

IN HIGHER LATITUDES,
WHERE THE "... SUN
   SLOPES DOWN TO REST
   WHEN DAY IS DONE",
   IT OBVIOUSLY TAKES MUCH LONGER TO GET WAY DOWN
BELOW THE HORIZON. HENCE A MUCH LONGER TWILIGHT.

THERE IS ANOTHER REASON

WE ONLY GET TWILIGHT AT ALL BECAUSE THERE IS A CERTAIN
AMOUNT OF MURKINESS IN THE ATMOSPHERE. IF THE ATMOS-
PHERE WERE CRYSTAL CLEAR, IT WOULD GET DARK AS SOON AS THE
SUN DIPPED BELOW THE HORIZON.
     IN THIS PART OF THE WORLD, THE ATMOSPHERE IS GENERALLY
VERY CLEAR, HENCE OUR SHORT TWILIGHTS.
     SOMETIMES, WHEN WE GET MOIST OR CLOUDY WEATHER, WE TOO
GET LONGISH TWILIGHTS.

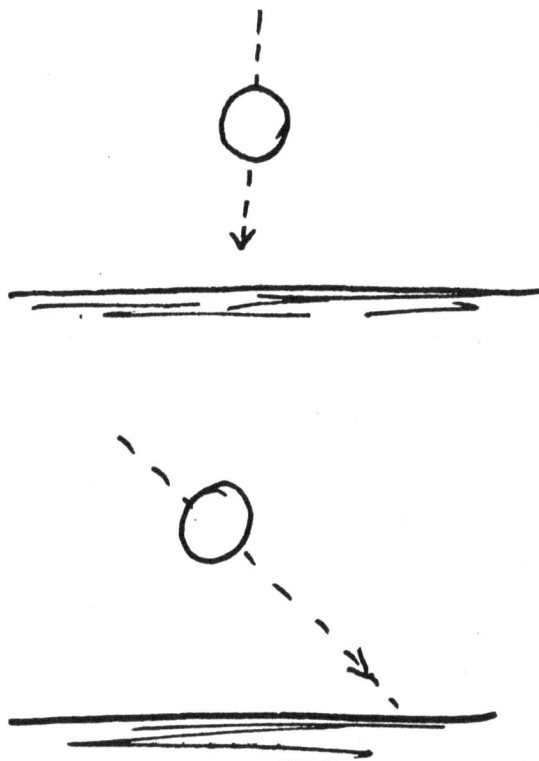

HISTORY

THE CARIBBEAN ISLANDS ARE A GOOD PLACE FROM WHICH TO REFLECT ON EARLY AMERICAN HISTORY.

IN THE EARLY COLONIAL DAYS, THE VARIOUS COLONIES OF ENGLISH AND FRENCH PEOPLE WHICH LAY SCATTERED ALONG THE EASTERN SEABOARD OF THE CONTINENTAL MAINLAND, AND THOSE IN THE ISLANDS FURTHER SOUTH, DID NOT DIFFER MATERIALLY FROM EACH OTHER IN WEALTH, STATUS OR CULTURE.

GEORGE WASHINGTON, AN OFFICER IN THE BRITISH ARMY, WAS STATIONED IN BARBADOS FOR SOME TIME AND FOUND IT VERY ELEGANT AND LIKE HIS HOME IN VIRGINIA. ALEXANDER HAMILTON, SON OF A BRITISH PLANTER IN NEVIS, WAS NO COUNTRY BUMPKIN WHEN HE GRAVITATED TO ANOTHER ENGLISH COLONY IN NEW YORK.

THEY WERE ALL VERY ALIKE THEN, AND THE POINT I AM TRYING TO MAKE IS THAT IT IS PROBABLY MUCH EASIER NOW TO VISUALISE COLONIAL AMERICA BY STUDYING THE CARIBBEAN ISLANDS, WHICH HAVE HARDLY CHANGED IN THE MEANWHILE, THAN IT IS TO VISUALISE IT IN AMERICA ITSELF, WHICH HAS CHANGED SO VASTLY IN THE INTERVENING 200 YEARS.

THE GREAT WORLD CONFLICT OF THE 18TH CENTURY BETWEEN ENGLAND AND FRANCE SOMEWHAT RESEMBLED OUR PRESENT DAY CONFLICT BETWEEN THE U.S.A AND RUSSIA. FRANCE WANTED TO UNITE EUROPE UNDER FRENCH LEADERSHIP: ENGLAND PREFERRED THE STATUS QUO.

AS IN OUR PRESENT DAY, THIS WAS THE PRIME MOTIVE OF THE WORLD CONFLICT, BUT MANY OF ITS BATTLES WERE FOUGHT IN FAR DISTANT COUNTRIES. IN OUR PRESENT DAY, THE BATTLES HAVE BEEN FOUGHT IN KOREA AND VIETNAM. IN THE 18TH CENTURY, MANY OF THE BATTLES WERE FOUGHT IN THE INDIAN OCEAN AND AROUND THE COLONIES IN AMERICA AND THE WEST INDIES.

IN BOTH CENTURIES THE FATE OF THE PEOPLE IN THE COUNTRIES FOUGHT OVER, ALTHOUGH IMPORTANT TO THEMSELVES, WAS SECONDARY TO ITS INFLUENCE ON THE MAIN OBJECT OF THE CONFLICT. THE 13 COLONIES OF ENGLISHMEN IN NORTH AMERICA MAY HAVE GOT THEIR INDEPENDENCE AND COUNTLESS MILLIONS IN INDIA MAY HAVE BEEN UNITED UNDER THE BRITISH CROWN BUT THESE FACTS WERE THEN CONSIDERED SECONDARY. FOR GOOD OR ILL, ENGLAND WON AND PRESERVED THE STATUS QUO. 40

HISTORY (CONTINUED)

THE SUBSEQUENT EFFECTS ON THE PEOPLE OF THE COUNTRIES FOUGHT OVER IN THESE FAR-FLUNG BATTLES WERE SOMETIMES MORE FAR-REACHING THAN THE OBJECTS OF THE MAIN CONFLICT ITSELF (A POINT WORTH REMEMBERING IN OUR PRESENT DAY).

A GOOD EXAMPLE OF THIS IS PROVIDED BY TWO NAVAL BATTLES FOUGHT IN THIS PART OF THE WORLD IN 1781 AND 1782. THE SAME TWO FLEETS WERE ENGAGED, THE FRENCH UNDER DE GRASSE AND THE BRITISH UNDER RODNEY. EACH LOST HIS MATCH ON HIS "HOME GROUND". RODNEY LOST OFF THE CHESAPEAKE AND DE GRASSE LOST OFF THE FRENCH ISLANDS IN THE WEST INDIES (BATTLE OF THE SAINTES). ALL SQUARE FROM A STRICTLY NAVAL POINT OF VIEW.

BUT CONSIDER THE AFTER-EFFECTS. AFTER THE BATTLE OFF THE CHESAPEAKE, CORNWALLIS WAS CUT OFF AT YORKTOWN AND WAS DEFEATED BY WASHINGTON AND LAFAYETTE. THE U.S.A. WAS LAUNCHED ON ITS METEORIC CAREER.

AFTER THE BATTLE OF THE SAINTES, JAMAICA WAS SAVED AND THE WEST INDIAN ISLANDS BECAME PREDOMINENTLY BRITISH.

BUT TO RETURN TO THE ORIGINAL POINT. IN ITS EARLY STAGES WEST INDIAN HISTORY AND AMERICAN HISTORY ARE ONE AND THE SAME THING. BUT HERE YOU CAN VISUALISE IT EASILY SINCE THE SURROUNDINGS HAVE REMAINED PRACTICALLY UNCHANGED. YOU CAN RE PEOPLE ENGLISH HARBOUR IN YOUR MIND WITH 18TH CENTURY SEAMEN AND SHIPS. YOU CAN "DISCOVER" THE FORTIFICATIONS ON UNION ISLAND, CANNON AND ALL, BY HACKING YOUR WAY THROUGH SCRUB. YOU ANCHOR UNDER THE LEE OF FORT ST LOUIS IN MARTINIQUE WHERE THE FRENCH SHIPS OF THE LINE USED TO LIE AND YOU CAN SWIM OFF PIGEON ISLAND WHERE RODNEY KEPT HIS CARRIER PIGEONS.

WINDWARD AND LEEWARD ISLANDS.

THE FIRST ARRIVALS IN THIS AREA WERE SAILORS, AND IT WAS NATURAL TO THEM TO DESCRIBE THE POSITION OF THE ISLANDS IN RELATION TO THE DIRECTION OF THE WIND, SPECIALLY HERE, WHERE IT IS CONSTANT.

THEY WERE SPANIARDS, SO THEY DESCRIBED AS "SOTTOVENTO" (LEEWARD) THE BIG ISLANDS FROM PUERTO RICO WESTWARD.
THE REMAINDER WERE "BARLOVENTO" (WINDWARD), AND VERY MUCH SO TO A SAILOR BEATING UP TOWARDS THEM.

MUCH LATER, WHEN BRITISH POLITICIANS WERE ORGANISING THEIR POSESSIONS INTO ADMINISTRATIVE GROUPS, THEY ADOPTED THESE TRADITIONAL AND PICTURESQUE NAMES. BUT THEY APPLIED THEM TO TWO GROUPS OF ISLANDS WHICH LIE ACROSS THE WIND. SO THE NAMES BECAME MEANINGLESS FROM A SAILOR'S POINT OF VIEW. SO PLEASE PRONOUNCE THE NAME LEEWARD JUST AS IT IS SPELT, AND NOT AS IT IS PRONOUNCED IN THE NAUTICAL LANGUAGE (LOO'ARD)

UNTIL THE END OF THE '50s THERE WAS A GOVERNOR OF THE LEEWARD ISLANDS WITH HIS GOVERNMENT IN ANTIGUA AND REPRESENTATIVES IN THE OTHER ISLANDS. IN FACT THE LEEWARDS WERE FEDERATED.

THERE WAS ALSO A GOVERNOR OF THE WINDWARD ISLANDS WHO LIVED IN GRENADA. BUT HIS ISLANDS ALL HAD SEPARATE GOVERNMENTS OF THEIR OWN, AND HE WAS THE GOVERNOR OF EACH SEPARATELY.

BOTH GOVERNORSHIPS WERE ABOLISHED IN 1958 AS A PART OF THE PREPARATION FOR WEST INDIAN FEDERATION — WHICH NEVER MATERIALISED. THE NAMES LINGER ON BECAUSE THEY ARE SO CHARMING, BUT BY NOW THEY HAVE LOST ALL GEOGRAPHICAL, NAUTICAL AND POLITICAL MEANING.

THE DUTCH USE THESE TWO NAMES AS WELL. STATIA, SABA AND THE DUTCH HALF OF S' MARTIN ARE DESCRIBED AS THE "WINDWARD GROUP OF THE NETHERLANDS ANTILLIES." CURACAO, ARUBA AND BONAIRE BEING THE LEEWARD GROUP. THIS MAKES SENSE ON ITS OWN, BUT PUTS THE DUTCH WINDWARDS IN THE MIDDLE OF THE BRITISH LEEWARDS.

THE FRENCH DO NOT USE THESE TWO WORDS TO DEFINE THEIR ISLANDS.

The End

www.shipyardpress.com